Authentic Antique Stenciling

Gen Ventrone

Schiffer Publishing Ltd

1469 Morstein Road, West Chester, Pennsylvania 19380

Printed in the United States of America.
ISBN: 0-88740-140-6
Published by Schiffer Publishing Ltd.
1469 Morstein Road, West Chester, Pennsylvania 19380

This book may be purchased from the publisher.
Please include $2.00 postage.
Try your bookstore first.

Contents

Introduction 5

Chapter 1 **Supplies and Preparation** 8

    Buy supplies 7

    Make a cutting box 8

    Prepare the Surface 9

    Practice Surfaces 9

    Preparing Tin 10

    Preparing Wood 11

    Preparing Special Surfaces 11

    Make a velvet palette 12

Chapter 2 **Copying and cutting the stencil** 14

Chapter 3 **Applying the Designs** 22

Chapter 4 **Applying Colors to the Designs** 26

Chapter 5 **Multiple Stencils for Tin or Furniture** 30

Chapter 6 **Other Stenciling Techniques** 54

    Stenciling on glass 54

    Stenciling on Velvet—Theorem Painting 58

    Stenciling on Walls 64

Chapter 7 **Stencil Designs** 69

    Flowers 69

    Leaves 71

    Veins and fine lines 72

    Fruit 73

    Borders 74

    Chair Parts 79

    Tray designs 96

4

Introduction

Stenciling has a long and ancient history, as old as art itself. It was a medium used by many famous artists throughout the world. Michelangelo marked the ceilings of the Sistine Chapel with stencils for guides, and Picasso is known to have incorporated stencils into a painting when he felt the need for it.

An ancient stenciler said, "It's a process known to everyone and as old as the need to which it responds."

Unfortunately, in modern day America, where everything from food to funerals is quickie and instant, the authentic methods of stenciling are known to but a few hundred experts and their fortunate students.

Well past ripe old, middle age, I went on educational television and taught the authentic methods of stenciling in six basic lessons. I could not possibly reach all the people who want to know more. My mail and phone calls tell me my would-be students are legion.

Therefore, for all those who want to know, this book is devoted entirely to the correct ways to stencil. Read carefully and thoroughly, and follow the directions and you will accomplish what our Early American ancestors did when they stenciled Hitchcock Chairs, Boston Rockers, trays and other tin or wood objects.

Authentic antique stenciling was always taught with precise instruction to long-suffering apprentices. It did not originate as "folk art" in the kitchens of long ago when ladies had "so little to do" that they had to find something to occupy their time. In fact, stenciling was a male-dominated field.

Stenciling was an artistic profession and was executed on walls, floors, tin, wood, fabric, papier-maché and glass. It is not "tole." Tole is a French word which means "sheet iron."

Right here then, in the beginning, let us forget "tole" and "folk art," because they are inexact terms when referring to Early American Decorative Art. We will speak instead of the material on which we are working be it tin, wood or whatever. We will call stenciling "art" because it is art when done correctly.

The art of stenciling is in the cutting. A child can be shown how to apply a stencil, a child could not cut one. The cutting requires a good eye and a love for perfection. As the Shakers said, "Trifles make perfection, but perfection itself is no trifle."

Students, either in my television audience or in my studio, are taught to study the hole that they have cut rather than the surrounding material. Develop your perspective, we all have it, we only need to bring it into practice.

When cutting a fine stencil, never cut a second hole until the first one is perfect. There is nothing more sloppy than a stencil cut in a hurry just to get it done. Once you have patiently cut a beautiful stencil you will want to cut more and more.

Although stenciling is as ancient as all art, having been found in ancient Egyptian and Chinese art, I am going to concentrate on Early American stencils. Originally, in America, stenciling was done on fine rosewood and mahogany furniture. Then, as mass production developed in our country, furniture was painted and hand grained to mimic the finer woods. Finally, when production reached frantic peaks in the nineteenth century, black, red, green, brown, yellow and off-white became the background colors of choice for stencil decorations.

The earliest American stencil designs were multiple-cut stencils assembled in baskets, bowls or in groups on the decorated piece. The use of the multiple stencil continued up into the Victorian period. After that, commercialism reared its head and stencils were all in one piece (one-cuts) and were put on everything—even sausage stuffers. As late as 1915, tin articles were being sold with one-cut stencils on them.

However, never did the beautiful hand cutting cease. Even in the one-cut period, the greatest care was taken to hand cut the stencil perfectly. The old time hand cutters would abhor the pull-out stencils being foisted on the public today.

Perfect cutting therefore, is what I wish to teach you first. Since the one-cut stencil is the simplest, that is where we will begin and work up to the more difficult and multiple stencil designs.

Chapter 1

Supplies and Preparation

There are five basic steps you will take to prepare yourself to stencil, and these are fully explained in the directions which follow.

Step 1. Buy supplies.
Step 2. Make a cutting box.
Step 3. Prepare the surface on which you will either stencil or practice.
Step 4. Make a velvet palette to hold lining powders, and make applicators.
Step 5. Copy and cut the stencil.

Buy supplies

The supply list:

½ yard architect's linen (or tracing cloth)	½ pint rust inhibitor (oil base)
single edged razor blades (industrial blades)	½ pint oil base, slow drying, high gloss varnish
masking tape	½ pint oil base flat black paint
Crow quill pen & India ink or a good drawing pen (Rapidiograph or something similar) with a fine point	paint thinner or turpentine
	metallic powders (a vial each of):
	rich gold lining
silver Crayon pencil	silver or aluminum lining
article on which you will stencil	copper lining
oil paints in tubes: Alizarin crimson	ruler
Prussian blue	scissors
Indian Yellow	¾ yard cotton back upholster's velvet for palette
raw umber	small bottle household ammonia to clean crow quill pen
burnt umber	
titanium white	palette knife
Japan oil paint: chrome yellow medium	cardboard (posterboard or Duro Glo) for mounting
American vermillion (optional)	patterns
brushes: 1½-inch brush for flat black, and rust inhibitor	#600, 3M Wet & Dry Trimite sandpaper
1½-inch soft bristle brush for varnish or use poly (synthetic) brushes	raw linseed oil
	rottenstone
sword striper #1	rubber dam punch (a dental tool)
square tipped quills, #1, #2, #3	leather punch
	notebook punch

Make a cutting box

Light Box

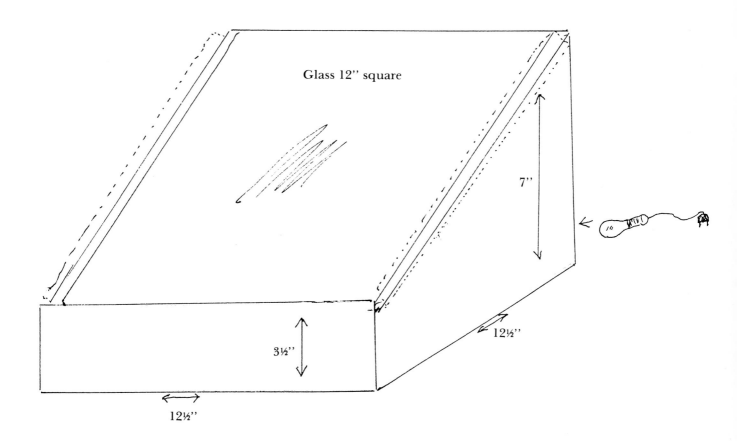

Glass 12" square

7"

3½"

12½"

12½"

To make the cutting box use four pieces of ¾-inch pine or some other inexpensive wood and one piece of 12" x 12" glass.

Construct the sides, front and floor of the box with the wood but leave the back open for ventilation. Nail ⅛-inch lath along the tops of sides and bottom of the box to hold the glass in place. Mount a 15-watt light bulb inside the box. Back the glass with tracing paper so that you will not be looking directly at the light bulb when working.

Practice Surfaces

Always practice stenciling on poster board, black Contact paper glued on cardboard or Duro Glo first.

The last two practice surfaces mentioned have sealed surfaces and need no preparation prior to varnishing. Poster board is very absorbent and must be sealed to accept varnish. Give the posterboard a coat of shellac and let it dry.

With your silver pencil outline on the working surface the area you will stencil. If you are doing a tray, turn the tray upside down on the surface and draw around the tray with the silver pencil. You will practice stenciling within these lines.

Preparing Tin

Sandpaper the tin to remove all rust, and then give the tin two coats of rust inhibitor. There are several good brands of rust inhibitor on the market. Let each coat of rust inhibitor dry for twenty-four hours then sand it down with dry fine sandpaper. Be sure to remove all ridges and sand between each coat. Give the tin two coats of flat oil base black paint over the rust inhibitor. Allow each coat to dry for twenty-four hours, and for a beautiful smooth finish be sure to sand between each coat with very fine sandpaper. The tin surface should now be ready to accept varnish for stenciling.

(Your paint store will tell you that you do not need a rust inhibitor and oil base paint. In the old days we did not get this argument but today we do. Therefore I advise my students that if the paint store insists that they are correct, ask how many antique trays they have restored. That stops the argument every time.)

Photo courtesy of the H.S.E.A.D., Inc.

Preparing Wood

First, clean the wood of all old paint. Give the wood two coats of flat oil base paint. Allow each coat to dry for twentyfour hours, and sand between each coat. The wood should be ready to decorate.

Preparing Special Surfaces

Refer to Chapter V of this book to prepare other special surface such as walls, fabric and glass.

Photo courtesy of the H.S.E.A.D., Inc.

Photo courtesy of the H.S.E.A.D., Inc.

Make a velvet palette

Fold an 18" x 20" piece of velvet in half lengthwise with the right side out. Bind all three edges with seam binding or overcasting. Your palette should now measure 18" x 10".

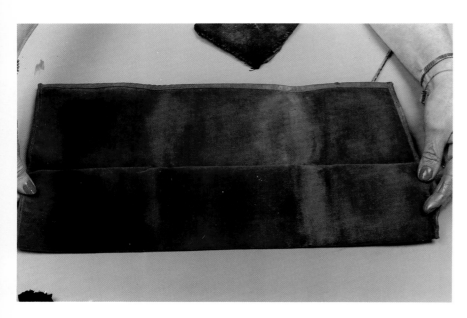

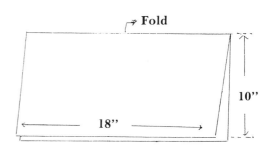

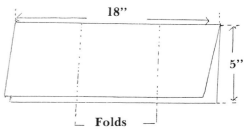

Using a palette knife take approximately half a teaspoon of gold lining powder from the vial, lay it down carefully half way up on the palette, then down to the bottom. About 2½ inches away, lay down the same amount of copper powder and then the silver powder. The rest of the palette can be used for any other lining powder you may purchase.

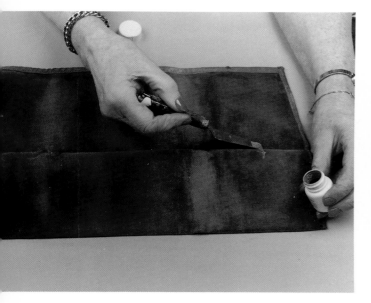

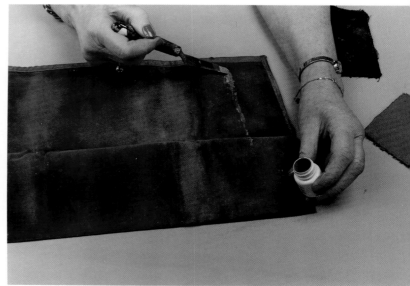

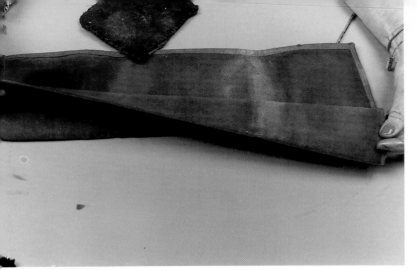

To store the palette, fold the top half over the powders so that it measures 18" x 5". Then fold the palette in thirds for storage as shown above.

Cut the extra velvet into four-inch squares which can be used as applicators. Each applicator should have overcasting stitches on all four sides to prevent bits of fabric from getting into the area where you are applying the stencil.

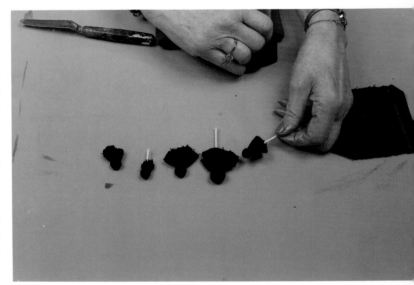

Much of the powder will be applied by wrapping these velvet squares around your fingers, but you will also need bobs of all sizes to apply lining powder to areas which are too small for fingers. To make a bob, wrap a bit of cotton around the tip of an old quill brush or any thin stick. You can even use a throat swab. Wrap a piece of the velvet (or very fine chamois) over the cotton and wire or tape it to the stick.

Now you have prepared all of your materials and are ready to advance to the fifth and last basic step before you do a stencil. Step five is the subject of the next chapter—Copying and Cutting the Stencil.

Chapter 2

Copying and cutting the Stencil

To copy a stencil, first cut a piece of architect's linen (tracing cloth) large enough to allow 1½'' surplus of linen beyond the lines of the design you have chosen to copy.

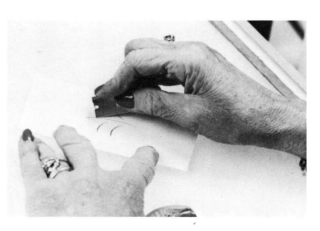

Place the linen over the design you are copying with the dull side up, and hold it in place with bits of masking tape.

Using your light box, a crow quill pen and black India or drawing pen and no-clog ink, copy the entire design or each piece if the design is multiple. Use care and precision. In this example, I am copying a leaf. Most stencil cutters use magnifiers for this intricate work.

Draw the thinnest lines (such as leaf veins) as one single line. Use circle templates, French curves or any other aid that will help you toward perfection.

Cutting Fine Lines in Stencils

Cut on the glass of your cutting box. If you make an error, cover it with transparent tape and cut it again. Cut one side of the fine line by inserting the point of the blade into a point (top or bottom) of the line.

Cut to the other end, cutting with one hand and moving the stencil with the other.

Turn the stencil piece to insert the blade at the opposite end from where you began and cut off a mere sliver of the material.

Examine it, hold it up to the light and look for imperfections. Cut away any errors carefully.

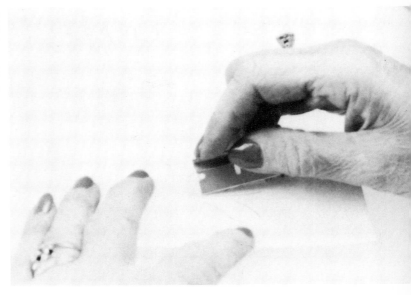

Cutting Leaf Stencils

There are all shapes and sizes for leaves. Insert the blade into the point of the leaf, and cut toward the center. Go back to the point and cut the other side toward the center.

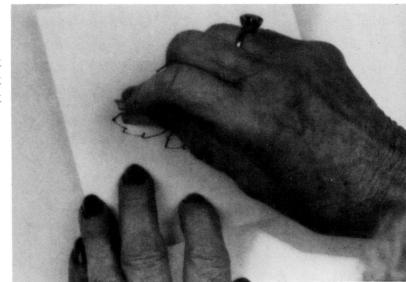

Cut each point this way and your leaf will have very sharp outer and inner points. Do not cut an "X" at the points. The petal type leaf is simple to cut. Just cut from point to point, examine and remove the angles.

The rounded end of any petal, regardless of size, can be punched out either with a rubber dam punch, if the petal is small, or with a leather punch if the petal is large. If a leather punch is called for, hold an index card behind the linen, and punch through the linen and the card. After you have punched out the rounded part, cut the petal in such a way that the round edge runs smoothly into the straighter edge. Do not make the petal look like a keyhole. Criticize your work.

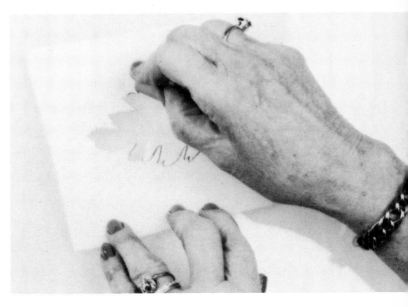

Cutting Flower Stencils

After you copy a flower in drawing ink, use your template and a lead pencil and draw a circle around the outer rim of the flower, the inner rim of large petals, the outer rim of the inside cup of the flower, and even around the inner most rim of the petals if there is room. These lines act as boundaries when cutting. Do not cut beyond these lines, and you will achieve perfect symmetry as was intended by the old time stenciler who originated the design.

When cutting a flower with pointed inner petals, treat them each as a leaf, cutting from point to point. On the rounded petals of flowers, you can punch out the top and cut the rest.

Cutting Fruit Stencils

Peaches, grapes and apples are always round. Always carefully check your cutting to be sure that there are no flat sides or angles. Slice away imperfections carefully.

Pineapples are made by cutting groups of rounded rectangles. Be sure to copy and cut the shape carefully. Melons must have the spaces between the sections cut evenly. Peaches are frequently cut into two sections. One part is a large circle or oval, and the other is a quarter moon.

Cutting Silhouette Stencils

When applying a stencil, the artist must keep the bronze powder within the stencil. When doing a silhouette however, the stencil powder is allowed to bloom outside of the stencil. Some call this "reverse stenciling."

You do not need an extra linen border around the design when cutting silhouettes. You can be skimpy with the linen here. Cut all of the parts of the silhouette—leaves, flowers etc., when you are finished, cut around the outside of the design to remove all excess linen.

Practice the cutting instructions given by cutting the following, and save the completed stencils for later when we begin to apply the colors.

These one-cut stencils were found on a tin canister.

The original of this small stencil was found on a miniature antique tin dustpan. It can be used alone to decorate a small article or group for a border. This stencil can also be grouped and shaded on a larger piece.

This more difficult design is very pretty, yet has the dubious distinction of originally decorating a sausage stuffer manufactured by Enterprise. This stuffer can be seen in the 1902 edition of the Sears Roebuck catalog.

This design can be used singly or repeated to form a border.

Now you have practiced the cutting techniques and are ready to apply your design to the surface you want to decorate.

Chapter 3

Applying the Design

In the examples we illustrate with these directions, I am working on a piece of black Duro Glo coated paper.

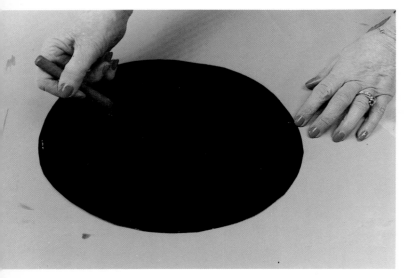

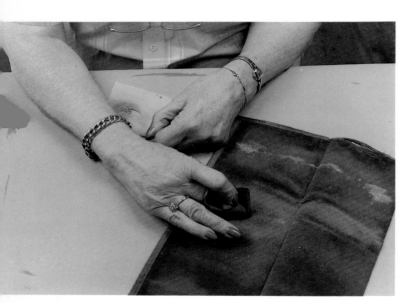

Varnishing the Surface

Varnish must be applied to the surface prior to stenciling. Never shake the varnish. Using your brush, apply the varnish with long, even strokes from side to side. When you finish in one direction, varnish in the opposite direction to be sure that every bit of the surface is covered.

Do not varnish too heavily or too sparsely, and spread the varnish a few inches beyond the silver pencilled area. Allow the varnish to dry to the point where it is tacky, but will not hold a fingerprint.

Another way to test for the correct tackiness of varnish is to lay a bit of linen on it. If the linen comes away easily, then you are ready to begin stenciling. But, if there is dampness under the linen the surface is too wet.

Ready to Stencil

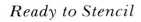

When the varnish is ready, open your velvet palette, and wrap either your index or middle finger with one of the velvet squares you have made. Keep the velvet smooth over the tip of your finger by holding back the excess with the thumb and other fingers.

Remember, the lining powder will go much further than you think. You can always add more powder to the design, but it is difficult to remove excess.

Place the cut stencil of the three small flowers from the miniature dustpan on the tacky varnished area outside of your pencilled line, and dip your velvet finger into the silver lining powder.

Rub off the excess silver powder either on the palette, newspaper, or on the back of your opposite hand as I do.

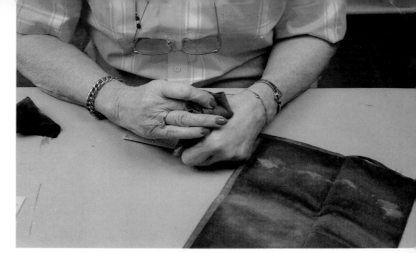

Polish the lining into the stencil in a circular motion from the outside to the inside. The polishing will remind you of finger painting.

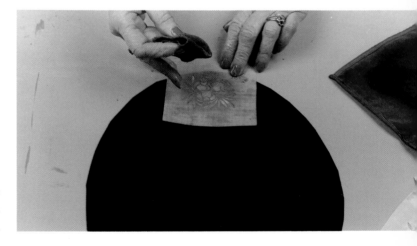

Polish round and round until you have covered every bit of the stencil. Add more powder if necessary. You are only testing at this point.

Lift the stencil and examine your work. If you used too much powder, the edges of the stencil will be fuzzy. Lines will be visible if the varnish was not applied evenly. If you are not pleased with your first attempt, do it again and again until you perfect the technique. Practicing will also show you how well your stencil is cut.

When you have finished applying the powder to the surface through the stencil, clean the stencil by placing it on a paper towel and wiping it with toilet tissue which was dipped into paint thinner. Dry your stencils before reusing them.

When you are ready to try a more complicated design, try applying the larger group of flowers in rich gold lining.

Remove the stencil carefully and examine your work.

Next, use gold lining to apply the round design you have cut.

Apply the basket of flowers for practice also in gold.

To give the flowers in the design a roundness, begin polishing in the center of the flower and move out to the points of the large petals.

A dark ring will begin to form. Let it remain, and it will give the flowers a more natural look. By applying the slightly varied amounts of powder to different areas of the design, you can create different appearances.

Shading

Shading is a technique we will use in more advanced multiple stencil designs later. To properly shade a single stencil for a group design, first apply the stencil in gold in the center of the surface you are decorating. Lift the stencil and place it to the top, bottom or either side of the first stencil. Place it so it overlaps a bit on the first stencil.

With powder, polish from the outside of the stencil to within a quarter-inch of the first stencil. Leave a dark area between the stencils, and this will make it appear as though it is behind the first.

Repeat this process all the way around the first stencil until the design reaches the desired proportions. Remember to always stay a quarter-inch away from previous stencils.

These stenciling techniques are basic to all forms of stencil decoration. Once you have become skilled at controlling the amount of powder applied, you can proceed to the embellishments of this basic style.

Chapter 4 *Applying Colors to the Designs*

Freehand Applications of Colors

The colors you see on stencils are not from colored powders as the uninitiated might think. These are actually oil paints applied with brushes. Allow the stenciled powders to dry for from 24-48 hours before trying to apply oil color. After it is dry, wipe the stencil with a cool, damp soft sponge or cloth. Dry the stenciled area, and then revarnish right over the stencil. Be sure to apply the varnish smoothly, and do not be rough with the brush on the design. My students prefer the poly brush for varnish because it is more delicate than a bristle brush. Allow this coat of varnish to dry for from 24-48 hours.

Washes—Transparent Colors

Washes are formed by mixing colored oil paints with varnish. To mix red, use alizarin crimson with a touch of burnt umber over gold. Use Indian yellow or yellow lake over gold or silver. Burnt umber is also sometimes used over gold. Prussian blue is mixed with varnish and used mainly over silver. Occasionally it is seen in a Sheraton blue on gold stencils. Prussian blue mixed with Indian yellow and varnish is green, and Prussian blue mixed with alizarin crimson is purple.

All of these colors are transparent, and the stencil will show through the color. If it does not, you have applied too much color. This color is easy to remove and repair because you have placed a protective coat of varnish over the design.

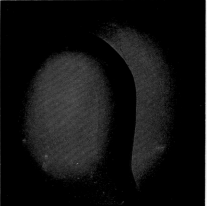

Opaque Colors

For brush strokes on stencils, you will need opaque paints called oils in Japan. Varnish is also used as a medium with these pigments. The beginner will need chrome yellow medium and American vermillion or sign writer's red. You can use the same brushes for opaque colors that you use for washes.

Application of Color

Practice your brush strokes on glass before attempting to apply colors to stencils. These techniques may help you to apply color beautifully to your stencil.

Never twist or attempt to control the brush, but rather let it ride easily along the surface. Hold the brush as you would a pencil, but a bit more upright. Work in a gliding motion, pulling the brush toward you and lifting the entire time.

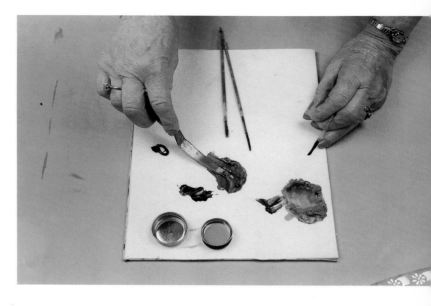

Place a small amount of the American vermillion on your palette, and pour a little varnish into a bottle cap. You will also need some paint thinner in a bottle for cleaning off the brush and the glass when you have finished.

Dip the brush into the varnish, and dress the brush on the palette. To "dress the brush" simply stroke the brush back and forth several times. Pick up some of the color on the brush and continue to dress the mixture until you have an enamel consistency.

Practice the "C" stroke first. This is the easiest stroke to learn. Lay the tip of the brush on the glass, and ease into a round head. Draw the brush toward you lifting all the while. The brush should come up to a fine hairline tail. The flatter down you lay the brush, the wider the stroke. For smaller strokes, use less pressure on the brush at the beginning of the stroke.

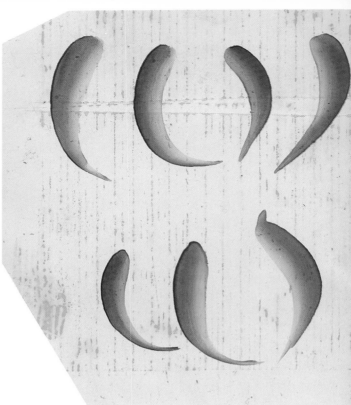

Practice several "C" strokes, then try reverse "C" strokes.

The "S" stroke begins on the knife or thin edge of the brush. Apply the paint to the brush as described above, and touch the thin edge of the brush to the practice area. Lay the brush down and stroke as you did in the "C", and draw the brush toward you to a fine hairline tail.

Begin a teardrop stroke the way you begin an "S" stroke, but do not lay the brush down as you would when doing a "C" stroke. Instead, hold the brush upright. Touch the thin edge to a practice area. Then push the brush down to the width stroke you desire. Again, draw the brush toward you and lift.

The "ric-rac" stroke is good for practice. The ric-rac stroke is an "S" stroke that is continuous, but instead of lifting the brush when the stroke is finished, do another immediately. Continue this up and down motion.

To paint stems or thin lines, hold your smallest brush up on its thin side, and pull quickly along the line toward you without applying pressure. Hold the brush straight up for the finest lines.

I use a sword striper for striping. The secret here is to mix a puddle of paint, dress the striper, and be sure that the paint is on the brush evenly. There should not be a drop of paint on the tip of the brush. Hold the striper between your thumb and forefinger. Use the other three fingers to guide your hand along the edge of the article you are striping. Then, pull the brush toward you and like Lot's wife, "never look back." Never look where you've been—look where you are going.

Remember these simple rules, and you will learn very quickly how to draw a very straight stripe.

Colors for Striping

For yellow striping and strokes, use chrome yellow medium (in Japan), raw umber and varnish mixed to a golden yellow. For green, simply add Prussian blue to the yellow, and use American vermillion for red.

Remember, varnish is the medium for this work. Your paints are always mixed with varnish. Do not waste your pigments. Place very small amounts on the palette, and they will go a long way.

How to Finish

After completing a design you must finish it properly to protect it. First, apply several coats of varnish to the design allowing 24-48 hours to dry between each coat. When a coat of varnish is dry, rub it down with wet 600 Trimite—a fine sandpaper manufactured by 3-M. Work gently in the first coats. Wash off all of the residue of the sandpaper, and dry the surface which should now appear grey. Revarnish when the surface is completely dry. Continue this process until there are no shiny pits remaining in the varnish.

The next step is to apply patina, especially if the design is on a tray. To make patina, mix ¼ cup of Rottenstone with enough linseed oil to make a paste. Add a few drops of household ammonia and a few drops of cider vinegar and mix.

Using a piece of a felt hat, a large powder puff, a large soft rubbing brush or a smooth cloth, rub this mixture on the stenciled surface round and round until you have a fine patina finish.

For chairs and other large objects which may be too time consuming to apply the patina, finish instead with an egg shell or satin-finish varnish.

Chapter 5 *Multiple Stencils for Tin or Furniture*

In multiple stencils, the design is made up of several parts which are cut individually. These individual designs may be fitted behind one another to make the design look rounded and to give some dimension.

Copy and cut multiple stencils as you would the simpler one—cut stencils always leaving 1½ inches of linen beyond the outline of the design.

In a multiple stencil, the most prominent piece is always placed first, and the other pieces are shaded behind it, one by one. This type of shading is also called "blooming."

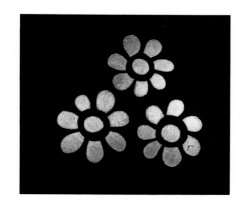

We will begin with a simple design consisting of three pieces: one leaf, a group of three small flowers, and a border piece. There is also some free-hand painting involved in this piece. Originally, this design appeared on an oval tray, but it can also be placed on a rectangle tray.

Prepare for stenciling just as described in previous chapters. Once the designs are copied and cut, apply the leaf with rich gold on the prepared surface.

Be careful not to apply too much powder, and polish in a circular motion from the outside of the stencil to the center. Do not bend the points of the leaves.

Lay the same leaf stencil half way over the first leaf and pick up some copper powder.

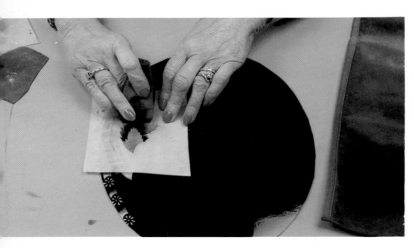

Rub off the excess powder, and begin polishing in the copper from outside of the points of the stencil and towards the first leaf.

Be sure to stay ¼ inch away from the first leaf and this will leave a dark area which will make the second leaf look as though it is behind the first.

Lay the same leaf stencil at the opposite end of the first leaf.

Use pale gold lining and apply the stencil carefully being sure to stay ¼ inch away from the bottom of the first stencil. Do not place the stencil down on the wrong side because the bronze powders on it will adhere to the tacky varnish where you do not want it.

Next, apply the group of three flowers next to the leaves, in rich gold.

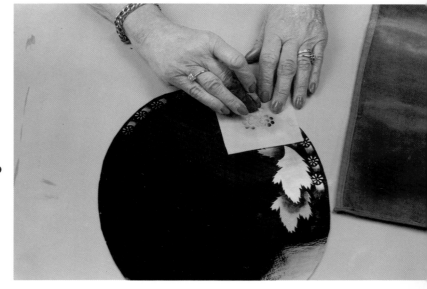

These are applied without shading.

The border is a simple piece applied over and over around the surface. Use silver lining and apply the powder from the flower to within a ¼ inch of the end of the stencil to make each piece look as though it is behind the other.

Repeat the designs until the tray is decorated as shown above.

Using the brush strokes and techniques you have already practiced, add some color to the tray.

Use green to accent the leaves and small flowers.

Color the veins of the leaves with brown. Once the design is painted and dry, use the finishing techniques you have learned to preserve the design.

The next stencil is a large basket of fruit. It is not one of the finer multiple designs, but if you accomplish it well, you will be the owner of an attractive tray.

I use this design to demonstrate and it fascinates audiences because of the great amount of shading involved.

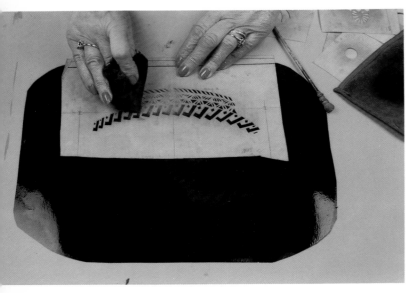

Once the stencils are copied and cut and the surface prepared, apply the basket in rich gold powder from the center to the ends. The centers of bowls and baskets should always be brighter than the ends to give the container a rounded look.

Next, shade in the bottom leaves of the pineapple as shown.

40

Next, place the pineapple in the basket. Do the top of the pineapple in silver and the rest in rich gold.

The pieces of fruit to either side of the pineapple are added next.

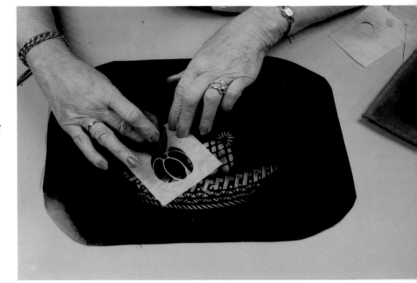

Remember to leave ¼ inch of shading around the pineapple and the basket.

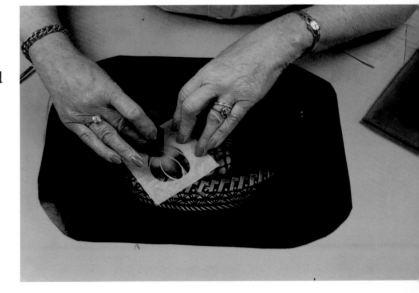

The more you practice shading, the better you will be able to judge exact distances for shading.

Shade the piece to the far right in gold.

Place the piece of fruit to the far left of the basket in silver.

Add the stem of the grapes to the right of the basket.

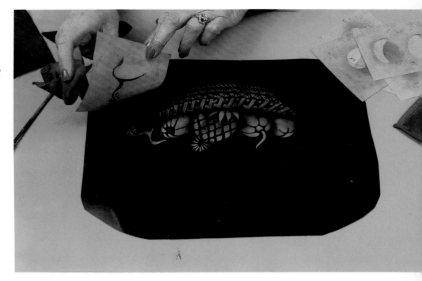

Next, add the grapes. There are two ways to shade grapes: from the outside of the stencil to within ¼ inch of the next grape, or the more attractive way of applying the powder carefully in the center of the grape and polishing round and round, or use a bob.

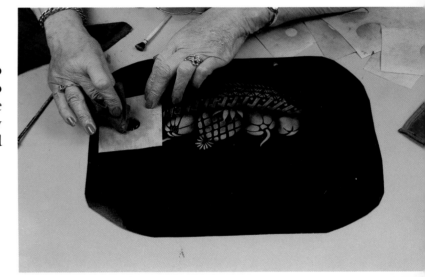

Never touch the outside rim of the stencil, and of course remain ¼ inch away from all other grapes.

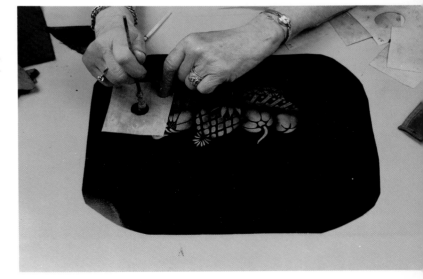

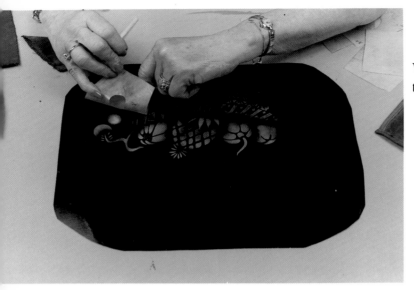

When you lift the stencil, you will see beautifully rounded grapes.

Next apply the fruit at the top of the basket.

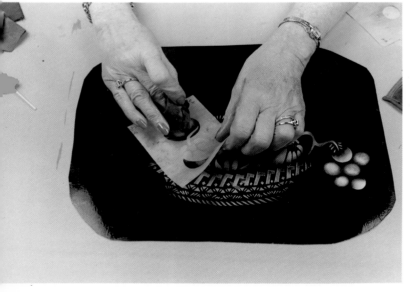

Apply the peach in rich gold lining. Be sure to polish the bottom in . . .

. . before the top.

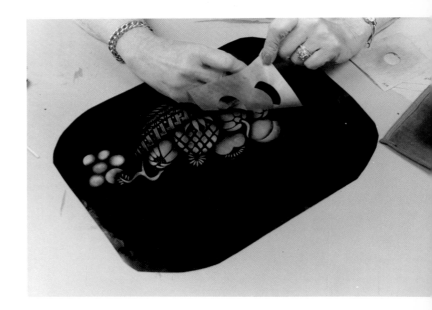

The strawberries are laid in reverse of what you might think. The part of the strawberry stencil containing the seeds (dots) is stenciled in first in silver.

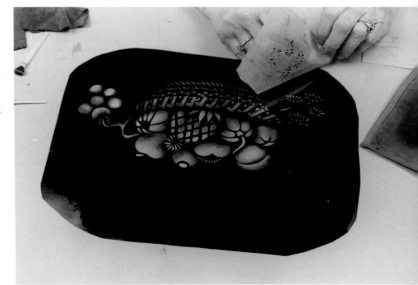

Lift the dot stencil off and place the rounded sections of the strawberries over the dots on the surface.

Polish just the edges of the strawberries with your finger or a bob in gold.

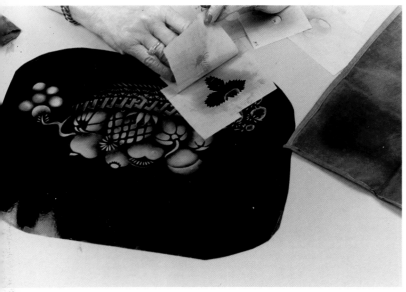

The strawberry leaves are stenciled next.

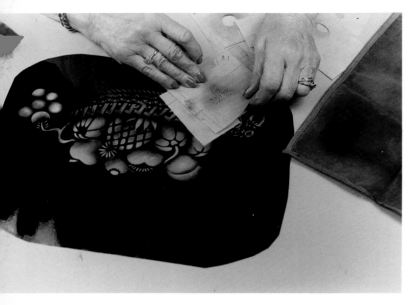

Polish in the veins of the leaves first, then . . .

. . . polish, in silver or gold, the edges of the leaves tapering off as you go.

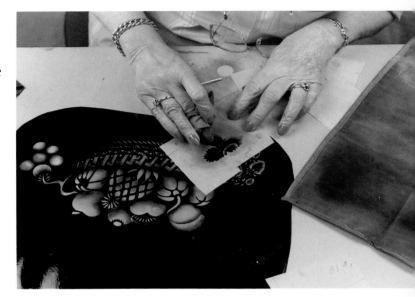

Place the stencil of the leaf directly behind the pineapple. Fit the veins of the leaf in and polish these in first right over top.

Lift the vein stencil and polish in gold or silver all around the edges of the leaves.

Stipple more gold or silver over the veins to soften the transition of color. To stipple, I use small, soft makeup brushes which I have cut straight with a razor.

Remember to leave a ¼ inch for the shading effect.

The sprays of small leaves are polished in last in silver.

Washing the Design

Wait 24 hours, wash, dry and varnish the design. Allow it to dry completely before beginning to add washes.

This design requires washes. Mix your pigments with varnish as described previously.

Mix alizarin crimson and burnt umber, and give the outside edge of the pineapple a wash of red.

Outline in red the piece of fruit to the left of the pineapple, . . .

. . . the upper or outer edges of the peach, . . .

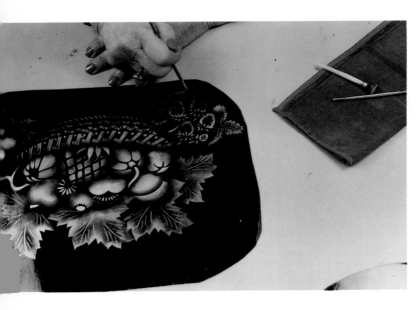

. . . and all of the outer gold edges of the strawberries.

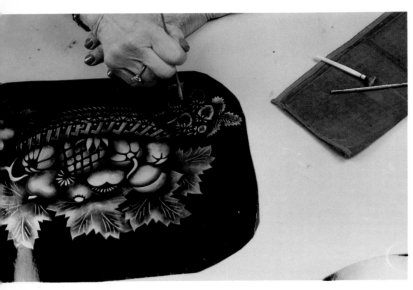

The strawberries are washed all the way around in one stroke for smoothness.

The piece of fruit above the pineapple . . .

. . . and the apple both have a very light wash of alizarin crimson with no burnt umber.

Wash yellow lake over the center of the pineapple, the two pieces of fruit on each side of it and over the center of the peach.

The small piece of fruit in the left of the basket is washed with a blue-purple of alizarin crimson and Prussian blue mixed and applied in a wash.

The last piece of fruit is also colored blue-purple.

The grapes are a very light purple.

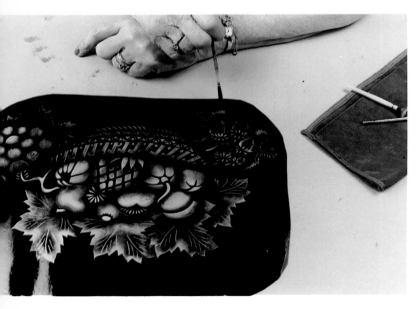

The strawberry leaves are washed with transparent green, . . .

. . . as are the center sections of the large leaves.

The sprays of leaves are alternately transparent yellow and green beginning at the left with yellow.

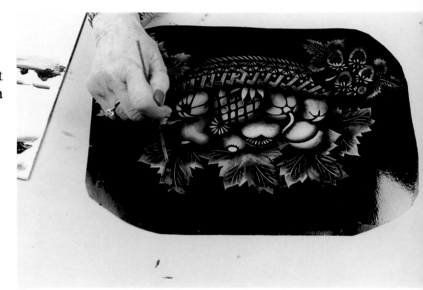

The completed stencil should be finished and preserved as described previously.

When applying a multiple stencil to a chair, varnish only the area which the design will cover. The directions for the placement of the design are the same as for a tray with the most prominent piece being laid first. After chair stencilling is finished, wait 24 hours, wash, dry THEN varnish entire chair.

You should now have a finished design which is ready to varnish and display.

Chapter 6 *Other Stenciling Techniques*

Stenciling on glass

Stenciling on glass is very much like stenciling on a tray or a chair, except you are working in reverse. Remember to cut the stencil beautifully, and all other rules apply.

To prepare the glass, first clean it well with Bon Ami, and rinse and dry it thoroughly. Blow the glass to be sure that all tiny dust particles are gone. Next, varnish the reverse side of the glass and another small piece for testing. Never test the piece you will stencil for tackiness because it will leave a fingerprint.

Let the varnish dry to the proper tacky stage in a dust free area. Some experts reserve a special drawer for this type of drying. When the varnish is dry, apply the stencil. Wait at least 24 hours before removing any excess powder with a soft cloth or sponge and cool water.

Paint the back of the glass you will stencil with any color you wish. Black, dark green and red are the best colors for this, and oil based paints work the best on glass. One Shot Enamel is made especially for glass and comes in many colors. Black is the simplest color to work with, but there is no rule which says that you cannot use other colors.

If you have a powder room window which opens into an enclosed or protected area, an interesting and attractive treatment is to do silhouettes on the glass and back it with colored enamel. You can also make silhouettes of either family members or famous personalities. These are suitable for framing.

The beautiful glass stencil presented here was found on an old clock, but it is so handsome that many people have just framed it and used it to decorate their walls.

After the stencil is dry wash the surface gently to remove any excess powder.

Next paint the central flower and the two small flowers above and below the large leaf with alizarin crimson and burnt umber at the edge. Allow this to dry.

On the following day, mix white, American vermillion and a touch of raw umber into a bright pink, and paint the background of the large central flower, the centers of both medium flowers, the buds and the small flowers. Allow this application to dry also.

Then mix white, raw umber and Prussian blue to a light blue and paint blue flowers. The other medium sized flower is yellow ochre behind the brown shading. Mix country green and paint in all of the green leaf. The background is old red which you can mix from American vermillion, black and varnish. Paint in the background except where the central flower is. This area is left open so that the movement of the pendulum could be seen in the clock.

Stenciling on Velvet
— Theorem Painting

You will need a few extra supplies for this work. Never use Japan paints on velvet, but all of the other paints you have may be used. The list below is only suggested colors, and it is not necessary to buy them all unless you intend to use them. Check the designs shown for the colors you will need.

The stencil or theorem for velvet painting can be done on several types of material. Many people use architect's linen (tracing cloth) as they do for trays and chairs. Some draw their theorems on plain brown wrapping paper. Neither of these would hold up under regular use, therefore I recommend drawing your design on the material and then covering each side of the design with clear contact. Then cut the theorem stencil, and this will give you a very strong stencil. Never use contact for tray and chair stencils.

There is one paper strong enough for theorem stencils, and your art store should be able to get it for you. This is White Waxed Stencil Paper #651 manufactured by the Bienfang Paper Company in Metuchen, NJ. There may be other companies which make a similar product.

Stencil paper is opaque and difficult to see through. Therefore, make a tracing of the theorem, tape it to the back of the stencil paper, put it on the light box and trace onto stencil paper.

This step by step explanation will not only help you to do the theorem shown here, but it will help you to look at any design and make it into a velvet painting or theorem.

Use tracing paper and your crow quill pen with drawing ink and make a complete tracing of the picture you wish to paint. In this case, we will use the basket of fruit pictured. You need not trace the veins, curlicues or markings on the basket.

Paint Colors

alizarin yellow	cobalt blue
Van Dyke brown	Cerulean blue
scarlet lake	crimson lake
brown pink	Italian pink
alizarin green	lamp black
raw sienna	chromium oxide green
Mars red	Davy's grey
cadmium red medium	thalo red rose
thalo blue	Venetian red
Paynes grey	

Other Supplies

stencil paper
stencil brushes #1, #2 and #3
#1 water color brush
Elmer's Glue
brush for applying glue
cardboard
cotton velveteen

Next, number the drawing using 1, 2 and 3, and in such a way that two areas with the same number do not touch. Areas with different numbers can touch. Some designs are numbered up to six, and the same numbering scheme applies. A numbered area must never touch an area with the same number.

After your theorem is complete, take the material you will use for stencil paper and draw, with a pencil, all of the #1 areas on one piece, all of the #2s on another and the #3s on a third until the theorem is complete. Next, cover each side with clear contact, then cut each piece as you would a stencil.

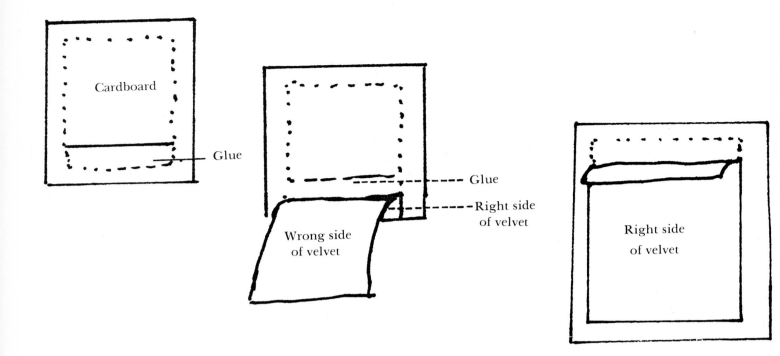

Beige velvet works best for background color if you can find it. Some stencilers dye white velvet in tea to make it look old. Many light colors make beautiful backgrounds particularly a very light blue which is a charming background for a rose.

Cut the velvet two inches larger all around than the design. Cut a piece of white or light colored cardboard or posterboard at least one inch larger than the velvet. If you are using stencil paper, it is usually large enough to cover the velvet, and you can work without a mat. With the back of your hand, determine which direction the nap of the velvet goes. Turn the velvet so that it goes away from you.

Draw a pencil line on the cardboard where you will lay the velvet. Then paint on two to three inches of Elmer's Glue at the bottom from side to side in a strip within your draw line.

Now lay the velvet, back side down, on the cardboard, and smooth it with the back of your hand. Bring the loose velvet back to you, and paint on three more inches of glue. Repeat this process until the entire piece of velvet is glued down smoothly. Save a scrap of velvet for testing colors before applying them to the picture.

There is now a product on the market called Quick Stick which is a self-adhesive mounting board. Velvet can be applied to it in seconds.

Place the colors you will use on the palette. Use stencil brushes for applying colors, but if you cannot find stencil brushes, you may use small squares of flannel folded in four. In this case, pick up the paint with the folded corner of the flannel.

Attach theorem #1 gently to the velvet with bits of masking tape or bankers clips. Apply colors from the outside of the theorem to the center getting lighter as you go. Do not be heavy handed. Remember, just as in stenciling, you can always add more color, but if you put too much on at first, you cannot remove it.

Apply the colors to the fruit as shown. When coloring the grapes, apply the paint just around the edges leaving a light spot either at the center or near the top of each grape. Do all of #1 before lifting the first stencil. Lift carefully, and set #1 aside to clean later with turpentine or paint thinner. Place theorem #2 over the area you just painted. You can study the tracing for correct placement, and proceed with the suggested colors. Lift and place #3, and continue applying the paint until all of the parts are painted in.

To bring the design together, wipe out almost all of the paint from the brush you used to paint the blue grapes and go over the grapes again with a very light touch. This will put some blue in the background. Do the same with the Sienna grapes, and carry the color up to the large leaf. Fill in any other open spaces the same way.

Dip the #1 color brush in the turpentine or paint thinner, and wipe off all of the excess. Pick up some chrome oxide green, and paint the curlicues as shown. Practice first on a scrap of velvet. Paint the veins on the leaves in the same way with burnt umber. The markings on the grapes and on the basket rim are also burnt umber.

You can place your initials somewhere on the painting with the water color brush. Before framing, allow the picture to dry for about two weeks.

Velvet paintings can bring out your creative talents. Copy any picture of flowers, fruit or animals and give it a try. Cats are fun and simple and can be done in two stencils, unless you have a background of trees and flowers.

Cut the eyes, ears, nose and the entire body of the cat on one theorem, and the head on the second. Use the colors of your own cat to brush in the background colors. Then with the #1 water color brush, paint in all of the details and lots of fur strokes to give the cat some realism.

Dogs and other animals can be done the same way. Use the water color brush for all of the freehand work.

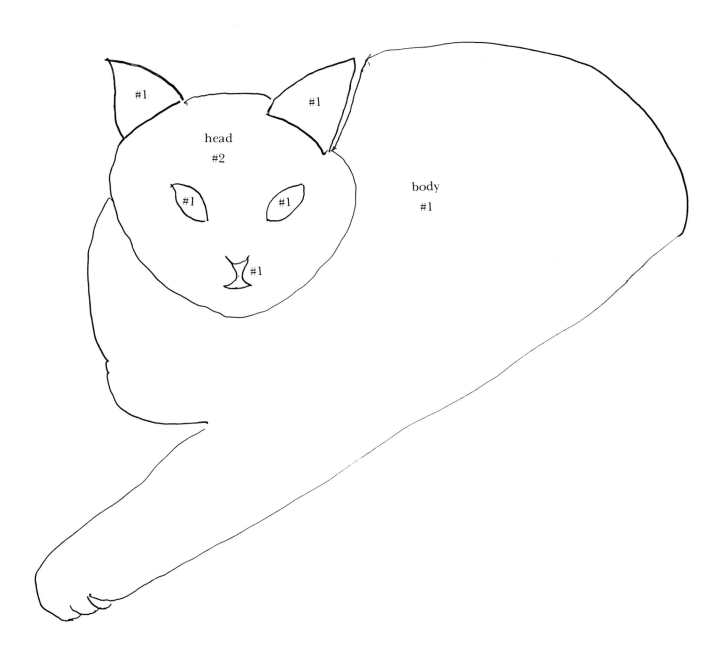

#1

#1

head
#2

#1 #1

body
#1

#1

Stenciling on Walls

The Ancient Chinese and Egyptians stenciled on walls making this technique one of the oldest forms of art. Wall stencils are seen in great abundance in churches and homes throughout Europe.

In Early America, stenciling was popular in homes, churches and public buildings and its popularity continued into the early part of this century.

Many of my students ask me how long a stencil will last on a wall. This question cannot yet be answered as ancient stenciling still exists. I can only say that it will outlast me.

Good background paint on the walls is essential to a fine wall stencil. There was a time when I would have insisted on four coats of good oil based paint first. However, once when we restored an old farmhouse and found we could only use sheetrock on the second floor because the house was not strong enough to support plaster—we found that latex was also a good background for wall stencils.

The stencil was very easy to apply to the latex, and the contractors assured me that it would take my stencils even though I had been using oil paints. I went ahead and painted on four coats of latex and stenciled with oil paints. I had no problems, and when it came to corrections, I even found that the latex covered better than the oil paint.

Over radiators the walls get particularly dirty, and after a time I painted in white latex over the dirt without touching the stenciled area. Would you believe you cannot tell where I retouched? If I had used oil paint, it would have shown a dividing line.

Therefore, even though this is an ancient art, do not be afraid to use the modern paints for the background, even with the oil paints for the stencils.

Supplies for Wall Stencils

clear contact	paint thinner
stencil paper	lots of toilet tissue
stencil brushes	and paper towels
water color brush #1	palette

Japan paints in cans or oil paints in tubes which will give you a greater color selection
Japan dryer or Penetrol

There are many other books which give examples of wall stencil designs, and I have included a few here for you to try. You can design each room to suit yourself and the way that you live, or you can copy an antique room. there are no hard and fast rules. *American Decorative Wall Painting 1700-1850* by Nina Fletcher Little and *Early American Stencils for Walls* by Janet Waring both contain examples of stenciling in antique rooms. Both books are available in soft cover and have exact pictures of Early American stenciling on walls.

Personally, I find the Early American look in wall stenciling too cluttered. When I see it, I picture the early artist throwing every stencil he owned at the walls. When I stencil a room today, I like to use borders near the ceiling and the floorboards, and then around the doors and closets.

If the room is very large with lots of wall space, then center designs on the larger walls are nice, or you can keep the large walls open for displaying theorems or trays that you have painted. The stenciled border on the walls serves as an excellent background for art.

Draw the wall stencil designs on the light table. Only use clear contact if you are using sketch pad paper. It is not necessary and will not hold on the waxed stencil paper. Before you cut, apply clear contact paper to both sides of the stencil, and then cut. If you are going to use a small stencil, this process should be repeated many time. Cut about twenty of the same stencil. Ten can be cleaned and drying while you use the other ten. if your design is a long piece, you may need to cut only half as many. You will, however, need more than one or two stencils when decorating walls.

Measure your room, and draw a plan of where you wish the stencil to be placed. Never dash ahead without a plan. It does not work. If the border is to go around the ceiling, measure how many times it will fit before you begin. It is wise to put a dot in the center of each stencil and use it as a guide.

Measure every area you will stencil, and draw the number of times the stencil will fit in each area on your master plan. It is better to have the stencil end abruptly at the end of the room than to have open spaces in the center of the room where you do not want them.

The Japan paints and oil paints are first mixed with a bit of Japan Dryer or Penetrol. I use small plastic containers for each color. Place the colors you will use on your palette. Next, lightly attach the stencil in place on the wall with masking tape. If you press the tape down too hard, you may lift off the base paint when you remove it.

Dip the stencil brush into a pigment and rub out all of the excess paint on the palette. Then, apply the paint to the wall through the stencil brushing from outside each hole towards the center. Again, remember not to be too liberal with the paint. You can always add more.

If you have a stencil for two colors, be sure to paint both colors before removing the stencil. For example, let's say you have a flower with leaves. You can apply the flower in red or burnt sienna, and the leaves in green. Do both before lifting the stencil.

When you have brushed in the color, lift the stencil gently, set it aside, and go on to the next stencil. Do not attempt to make corrections at this point. Complete the entire area where you are working and then clean all of the stencils. Then, while the stencils are drying, use your small water color brush, and paint over the errors with background paint.

Chapter 7

Stencil Designs

Flowers

Flowers

This bolster back design was found on the chair whose back design is on page 86.

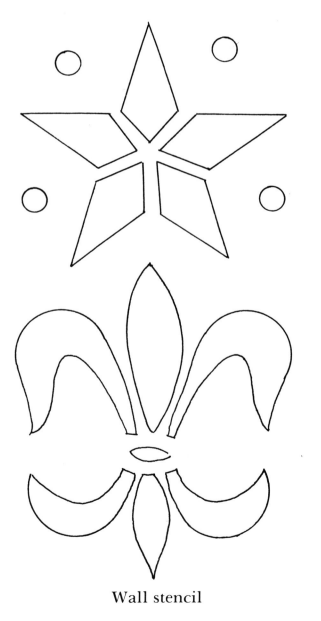

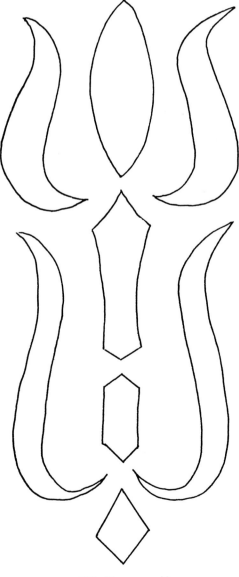

Wall stencil

Wall stencil

Leaves

Veins and fine lines

Scroll for rocking chair splat shown on page 94.

Fruit

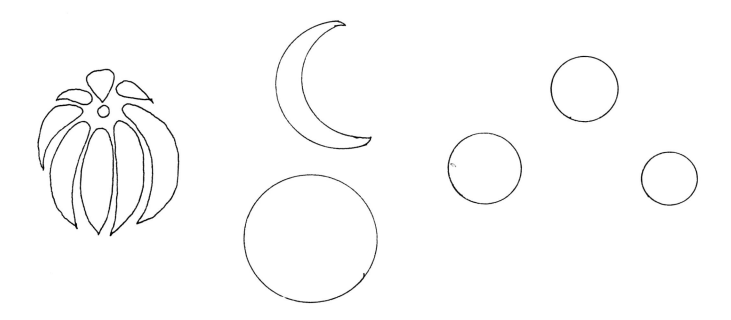

Photo courtesy of the H.S.E.A.D., Inc.

Borders

Wall stencil

This center splat design
was found on the chair
whose splat design is shown
on page 80, center.

Wall stencils

75

Borders

Wall stencils

Borders

Wall stencils

Borders

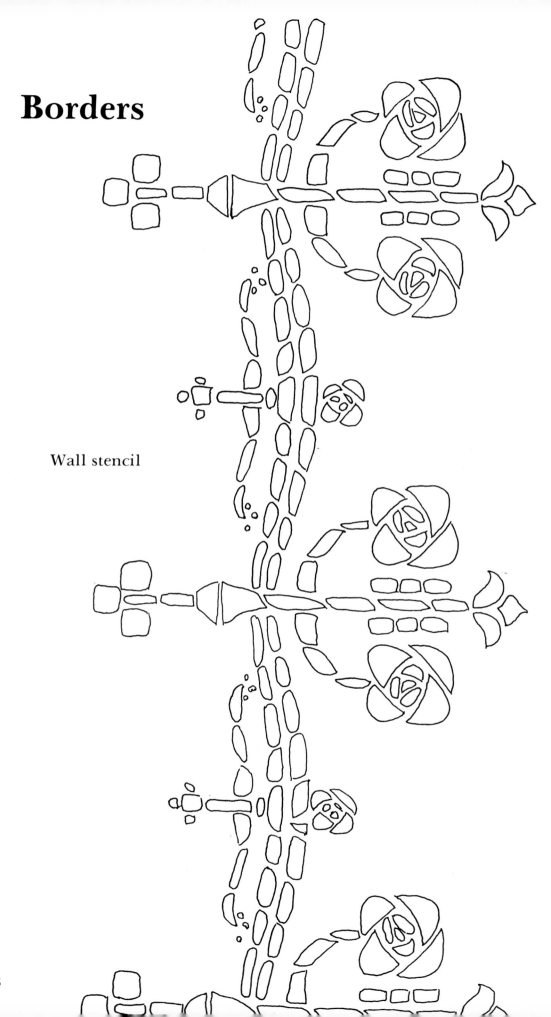

Wall stencil

78

Chair Parts

Top of chair stile

Center of stile

Bolster design

The three designs above were found on the chair whose splat design is shown on pages 92 and 93.

This stile design was found on the chair whose splat design is shown on page 86.

Chair Parts

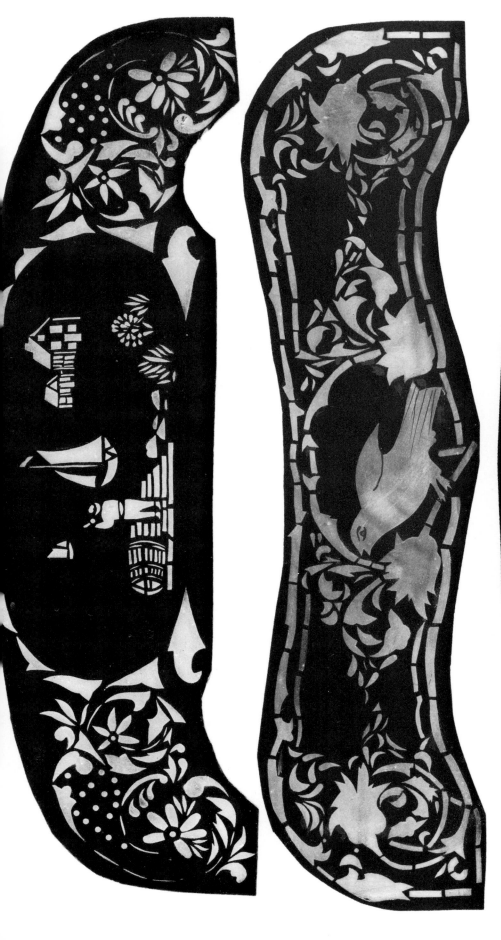

Chair Parts

Center splat

Designs for center splat shown above.

Chair Parts

Designs for center splat shown on page 82.

Chair Parts

Top splat found on the same chair whose center splat shown on page 82.

Designs for center splat shown at left.

Designs for the top splat shown on page 84.

Chair Parts

Designs for the chair back shown on page 86.

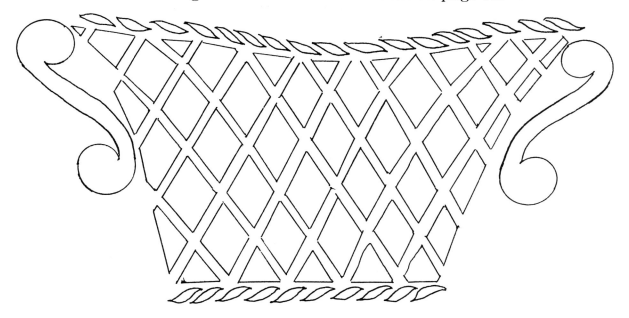

Chair Parts

Stencil designs used in the chair back on page 86.

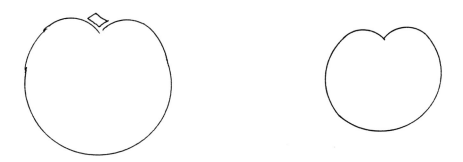

Chair Parts

Stencil designs used in the chair back on page 89.

Chair Parts

Stencil designs used in the chair back on page 89.

Chair Parts

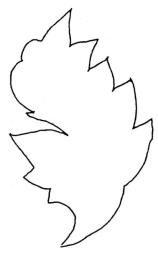

Designs for the chair
back shown at right.

Chair Parts

Designs for the chair back shown on page 92.

Chair Parts

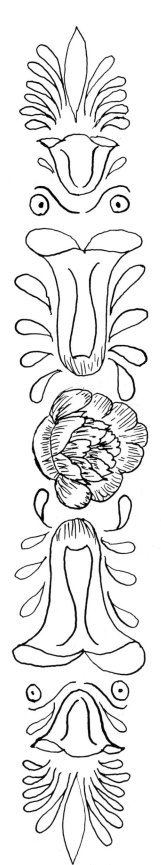

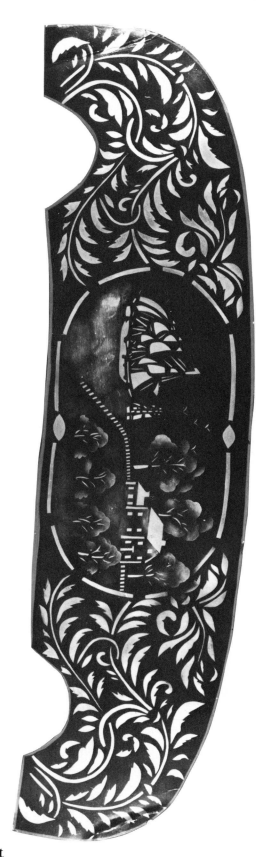

Seat roll design found on the chair whose splat designs are found on pages 82 and 83.

Designs for the rocking chair splat shown on
page 94.

The scroll design is shown on page 72.

Tray designs

Stencil designs for the tray shown on page 96.

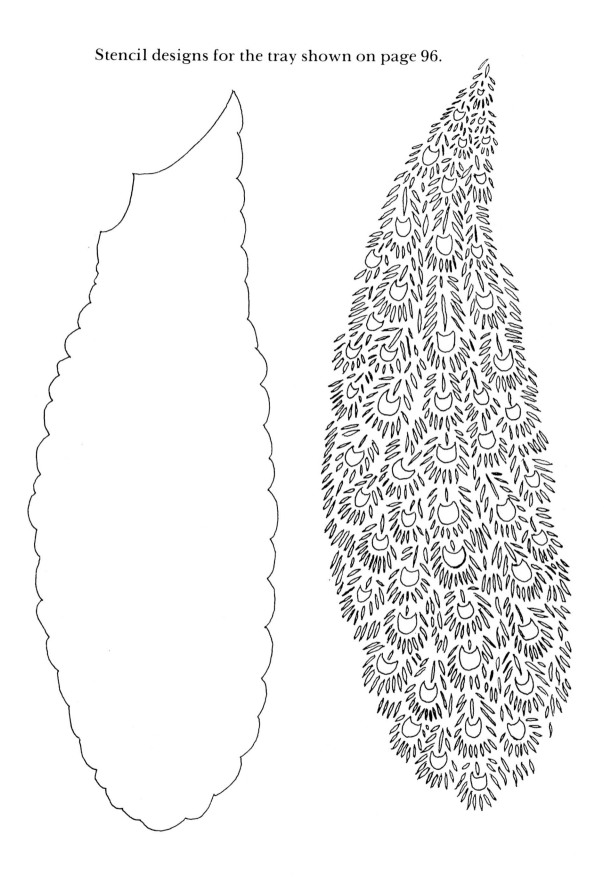

Stencil designs used in the tray on page 96.

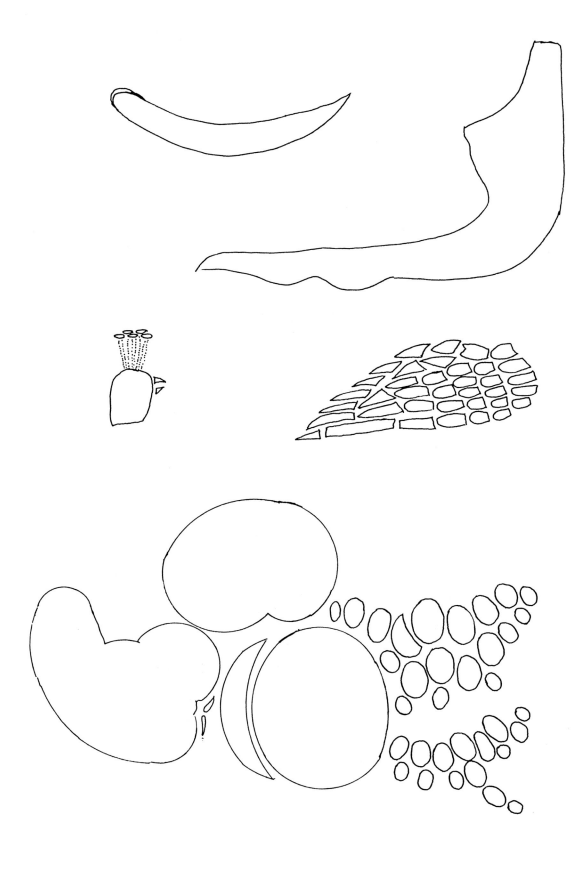

Stencil design for tray shown on page 100.

Stencil designs used in the tray on page 100.

Designs for the tray shown on page 104.

Designs for the tray shown on page 106.

Designs for the tray shown on page 108.